Green Manufacturing:
Paradigm Shift to Sustainable Capitalism

By Ade Asefeso MCIPS MBA

Second Edition

ISBN-13: 978-1500100339

ISBN-10: 1500100331

Publisher: AA Global Sourcing Ltd
Website: http://www.aaglobalsourcing.com

2

Table of Contents

Disclaimer

This publication is designed to provide competent and reliable information regarding the subject matter covered. However, it is sold with the understanding that the author and publisher are not engaged in rendering professional advice. The authors and publishers specifically disclaim any liability that is incurred from the use or application of contents of this book.

If you purchased this book without a cover you should be aware that this book may have been stolen property and reported as "unsold and destroyed" to the publisher. In this case neither the author nor the publisher has received any payment for this "stripped book."

Dedication

To my family and friends who seems to have been sent here to teach me something about who I am supposed to be. They have nurtured me, challenged me, and even opposed me.... But at every juncture has taught me!

This book is dedicated to my lovely boys, Thomas, Michael and Karl. Teaching them to manage their finance will give them the lives they deserve. They have taught me more about life, presence, and energy management than anything I have done in my life.

Part 1: Green Manufacturing

Chapter 1: Introduction

Manufacturing is when you take raw materials and combine the raw materials together to form a finished product. Most people when they think of manufacturing they think about having to order all of the numerous parts that are going to be needed to put together the finished product that is going to be for sale. For example, computers require a variety of little parts to be put together to sell the finished product. With manufacturing, you are probably aware of the various forms of manufacturing that can be used, but you might not be familiar with green manufacturing.

When people think of manufacturing they do not think of green manufacturing because the thought of manufacturing is large companies, putting numerous emissions into the air to manufacture their product. For example, chemical processing plants and gas refineries are types of manufacturing plants, which nobody thinks about them using green methods of manufacturing. The problem is that more and more people are becoming concerned with the environment, so more companies have to change their manufacturing methods to help protect the environment.

One thing that many companies are beginning to do to help their business go green is recycling. While many manufacturing plants have begun, recycling this is only a small step that they can take to go green. Green manufacturing is a viable option for all manufacturing plants because it is all about choices in the manufacturing methods that you use. Green manufacturing supports and sustains a renewable way of producing products and/or services that will not harm you or the environment.

One of the biggest concerns with manufacturing plants is that they are a big source of pollution and wasted energy. Manufacturing plants account for about 35% of the energy used each year in the UK. Aside from all of the energy, it consumes manufacturing often leads to pollution because most of the energy that is used in manufacturing is obtained via combustion processes from coal, coke, natural gases, oil, and waste which generate a lot of harmful greenhouse gases.

No matter what type of manufacturing you are doing, it is going to create some type of pollution because of the amount and type of waste that is produced. If your company is producing electronic items, you are going to have problems disposing of certain components because of the various depositions and etching technologies that are being used in making the components, the same holds true with chemical and primary material plants. Regardless of what industry you are, working is waste disposal and energy consumption is a major problem. This is where the concept of green manufacturing comes into play. By making, a few small changes you can help make your manufacturing plant more environmentally friendly.

Here are some things that you should know about green manufacturing

1. It uses raw ingredients (which can and does include organic ingredients if the pricing is reasonable) as much as possible if the finished product is biodegradable.

2. Does not use hazardous chemical conditioners, chemical anti-bacterial or chemical preservatives in any of the products that might end up in waste systems (landfills) or in the environment.

3. It provides a cleaner source of energy through new technology. This will decrease energy consumption.

4. It can convert pollutants and wastes into by products and promote their use and recycling along with the use of the product (such as ink cartridges).

5. It uses process improvements to maximize the yield and to help minimize the waste that is produced.

6. It can be expensive to convert from your previous manufacturing practices because it is going to involve numerous changes.

7. Finally it's much better for the environment and makes better use of the materials that are being used.

Green manufacturing has gone from being a trend in manufacturing to a cornerstone of the manufacturing industry. It has become apparent that the manufacturing businesses that are using green manufacturing are claiming more and more of their markets and showing that green manufacturing provides a high quality product.

If you are a business owner of a manufacturing company you should carefully consider green manufacturing. It is important to start considering an approach to the management of your supply chain that factor in green manufacturing. While it can seem overwhelming and daunting it is entirely possible to implement green manufacturing into your production process.

Here is what you need to know to do that

Know how green you really are: The first step in incorporating green manufacturing into your overall manufacturing strategy is to determine exactly how green your business really is. You need to have a clear understanding of exactly how your business spends and what your consumption process is since you won't know what to change if you don't know what is already going on. You will also need to have a clear understanding of just how green your supply chain is positioned.

Have a plan: Once you have a clear idea of how green your manufacturing business is then you can begin to devise a strategy on how to incorporate green manufacturing. You will need to create green manufacturing goals in a way that will allow you to track the progress of your business in using green manufacturing. These goals should be in written form and should be broken down into short, medium, and long term goals. You should also attach a time frame to each goal. When this is done correctly you will begin to see different green initiatives that can be used to broaden the green manufacturing within your business.

Appoint someone to be in charge: It is crucial to have a point of accountability. You will need to appoint someone who will be in charge of making sure that the green initiatives that you have decided are implemented within the company. Many manufacturing businesses have appointed a "chief sustainability officer" who is in charge of all green efforts. Whoever you appoint will depend on the size and type of your business and the industry that you operate in. However, it is critical to have someone who is in charge, accountable, and is empowered to make green change happen.

Start with the easy stuff first: Many times manufacturing business owners become overwhelmed at the idea of implementing green manufacturing. Keep in mind that there is no set order that you need to do this in. You can start with the easiest steps first and then add on from there. Keep in mind that you don't have to completely overhaul your supply chain in order to see gains from going green. You can implement smaller changes such as adding recycling and see a great cost savings right away. You can also make small improvements for better energy efficiency, reduce waste, or streamline paperwork procedures and see real gains.

Chart your progress: One of the most important steps when you are implementing green manufacturing is to chart your progress. You need to make sure that you are following what is happening and how the changes that you have put in place are paying off. This is the only way to make sure that the green manufacturing you are implementing is really making the changes that you have worked for. In addition, you should make sure that both your employees and your customers know of your efforts to implement green manufacturing.

Chapter 2: Why Green Manufacturing?

More and more manufacturing companies are turning to using green manufacturing. There are a number of reasons that they have chosen to do so beyond simply having a commitment to being environmentally friendly. Companies are finding there are a number of benefits to using green manufacturing and they must be aware of why it is important.

Here are some of those reasons

Manufacturing companies are listening to their environmentally aware customers: More and more consumer are seeing the benefits of purchasing green products and are become much more aware of environmental issues. These informed consumers are asking more questions about the things that they purchase. This has lead to many consumers actively seeking out products that are made in a green manufacturing process. Because of this many companies have begun educating themselves about green manufacturing and preparing answers for their customers about how green their manufacturing process really is, if their supply chain is green, how much impact are they having on the environment, and whether or not they recycle. It is crucial that if you use green manufacturing that you communicate that to your customers through your marketing message.

There is green involved when going "green": The bottom line is that manufacturing companies are interested in the bottom line. Many companies have quickly seen that their customer's interest in green products can mean an increase in their profitability. Studies have shown that there is a substantial link between an improved environmental performance and higher profitability. Manufacturing companies have looked closely at their supply chain and seen areas where improvements in the way they operate by using green manufacturing can produce profits.

Cost cutting is crucial: Using green manufacturing can be highly instrumental in cutting costs within the manufacturing company. Business owners are always looking for ways to cut costs and green manufacturing can be effective in making that happen. From the money saved by recycling to lower waste costs green manufacturing can improve the bottom line of any manufacturing company in a number of different ways.

Responsible manufacturing: While responding to customer's demands and making money is what keeps the doors open there are manufacturing companies that are interested in socially responsible production. These companies are turning to green manufacturing in an attempt to reduce their carbon foot print and make a product that does not harm the environment because it is the right thing to do. The other benefits of green manufacturing come along as a side reward.

It is important that every manufacturing company regardless of size or type becomes aware of the many benefits of using green manufacturing. Businesses can find that when they reduce the impact that their production processes are making on the environment they can find significant cost savings. Manufacturing companies that want to begin this process need to start by closely evaluating their supply chain. This includes every aspect from purchasing, planning, and managing the use of materials to shipping and distributing final products.

However, it is still surprising to learn that many manufacturing companies are still unaware of the potential benefits of using green manufacturing. Even with the public's focus on green products, that benefits that have been clearly detailed, and the increased profits that are the result many manufacturing business owners still have not begun implementing green practices. It is important to state that in addition to the benefits listed above using green manufacturing practices can result in; lower waste-disposal and training costs, fewer environmental-permitting fees, and reduced materials costs. Hopefully more manufacturing companies will turn to green practices when they begin to see the long term possibilities of using them.

Chapter 3: Ways to Start Going Green

It has been clearly shown that manufacturing firms that have gone green are finding that it saves them thousands of dollars each year. Going green will cut down energy costs, and can even save money on insurance rates. Experts predict that green manufacturing will be the most widely used manufacturing method within the next five years

Manufacturers should understand that if they decide to go green, it can begin in small and simply ways. The overall cost of going green is fairly negligible, for most companies.

Here are some ways to get started

Recycle materials: This is the simplest way to go green. Recycling is both easy and affordable to put in place. Manufacturing companies need to take a look at the products their company uses, and find ones that can be re-used at the facility. The bottom line is that recycling products within a manufacturing facility, will save any company considerable money. One of the most important aspects of recycling is to make sure that employees have access to recycling stations. An easy solution is to place bins around the facility, where employees can easily access them, to toss products that can be recycled. Rewards and incentives can also encourage them to use the bins, instead of just tossing there used items into the garbage.

Clearly identify the wastes: Another important step toward going green, is finding all the wastes, in the manufacturing process. Manufacturers should look closely at the harmful wastes and emissions, their business may be producing. Many manufacturers have made a switch to solar or wind energy, to cut down energy costs. In addition changing to organic materials can also cut down on harmful emissions.

Continue with regular training: In order for green manufacturing to be successful, it is critical that employees understand the importance behind going green, and recycling. Many manufacturers have found better success by offering incentives, to employees that regularly practice recycling and going green. Training can also help make sure your workers know where the recycling bins are, and what items are able to be recycled, and what the overall green manufacturing plan is.

Look at the manufacturing process: Manufacturers can also begin going green with their products, by looking at each one of them individually, and deciding how they can re-design them. Many manufacturers are also finding ways to build their products with natural materials, and look for machines that produce less waste.

Purchase only from green suppliers: Manufacturers, who are making an effort to go green, are also making it a priority to only purchase raw materials from green suppliers. This way they know that from beginning to end their product is green. Every aspect from the design to the packaging can be greened up in some way.

Manufacturing businesses should realize that while it will take an initial investment on their part to start going green, once they make the investment, they will start to see immediate and profitable results. Green manufacturing experts recommend that when looking at any product, manufacturers should use the three life cycles to design them. The three life cycles simply means designing a product for re-use.

1. In order to really be a green product once the product has gone through its life cycle, it needs to have at least some parts that can be recycled. Many manufacturers are trying to develop products so at least some of the parts can be recycled.

2. The other part of the three life cycles includes; developing a product that can be interchangeable with others. Green products are meant to be recycled and used again in the future or if perhaps if the product is not recyclable, it can be used for many years.

3. Additionally, instead of creating a new product, manufacturers can consider releasing additions or updates to the product.

Chapter 4: Guide to Going Green

Manufacturing firms that have gone green have found that it saves them thousands of dollars/pounds each year. Going green will cut down your energy costs and even your insurance rates.

Here is a simple guide to going green at your manufacturing facility.

Step 1 - Identify the wastes

The first step toward going green is finding all the wastes at your facility. Look at the harmful wastes and emissions your company is using to help you decide what you can fix. You can use solar or wind energy to cut down energy costs. Changing to organic materials can also cut down on harmful emissions.

Step 2 - Recycle materials

A simple way to go green is to start recycling. Take a look at the products your company uses and find ones that can be re-used at the facility. If you have empty plastic containers, find other places to use them. Recycling products within your facility will save your company money because you will not need to purchase new containers and other things.

Step 3 - Set up recycling stations

Another important aspect of going green is to have access to recycling stations. Place bins around the facility where employees can easily access them to toss products that can be recycled. Encourage them to use the bins instead of just tossing there used items into the garbage.

Step 4 - Hold regular training meetings

Staff members need to understand the importance behind going green and recycling. Offer incentives to staff members that regularly practice recycling and going green. Make sure your staff members know where the recycling bins are and what items are able to be recycled.

Going green will minimize the waste and the pollution for the entire planet. Going green not only will benefit the current generation, but future generations as well. You can start going green with your products by looking at each one of them individually and deciding how you can re-design them. Find ways to build them with natural materials and look for machines that produce less waste.

It may take an initial investment on your company's part to start going green, but once you make the investment, you will start to see immediate results. When you start looking at your products, use the three life cycles to design them. The three life cycle simple means you are designing a product for re-use. The products you design need to be recycled and used again in the future. Perhaps your product is not recyclable, but it can be used for many years. Instead of creating a new product, consider releasing additions or updates to the product.

Once your product has gone through its life cycle, it needs to have at least some parts that can be recycled. When you develop the product, try to develop it so at least have of the parts can be recycled. The other part of the three life cycle includes developing a product that can be interchangeable with others. This means the parts that are included in one product can be used in another product. Instead of customers tossing two products, they only are tossing one and using the parts from the broken one to keep the other product working.

Have a policy that states your products can be returned when they are old or broken. Use the parts from these products for other parts and look for ways to create new products using the parts from the old ones. If you need to purchase raw materials from other companies, try to only purchase them from companies that have gone green. Supporting the environment is the responsibility of everyone on the earth and when everyone works together, the planet will be safer and healthier for everyone.

Chapter 5: How to Set up Green Manufacturing

At one time it seemed like green manufacturing would only be a passing trend. However, today that assumption seems to be wrong. More and more businesses are turning to using green manufacturing. These manufacturing businesses are seeing that there is a multitude of benefits attached to using green manufacturing. In addition, these same manufacturing businesses are finding that they can claim an even bigger part of the market due to their green manufacturing. This means that manufacturing businesses that have not yet begun to use green manufacturing need to rethink their position and determine what green manufacturing principles they can put into their production process. The good news is that there is plenty of information to help you gets started.

Here is what you need to know about how to set up green manufacturing

Decide why you should do this: The first step in setting up green manufacturing is to decide why you are going to do this. Studies show that the manufacturing businesses that carefully consider this before implementing green manufacturing are much more successful at it. You will need to formulate what your goals will be in conjunction with green manufacturing. Keep in mind that attracting more customers won't be enough of a goal to make green manufacturing effective for your business.

Make a plan before starting: In order for your green manufacturing to work you will need to have a plan. You should take plenty of time to determine how you will not only implement green manufacturing but also how you will measure the effectiveness of it. Do not rush through the planning stage. Doing the right amount of research will be crucial for the success of your green manufacturing initiative. During this stage it can also be helpful to talk to other manufacturing business owners about their experience with green manufacturing.

Put a person in charge: If your green manufacturing is going to be successful then you will need to have someone who is accountable for the program. You can't implement green manufacturing and then just hope it works. Someone should be in charge of all aspects of the green manufacturing program. This person will responsible for making sure that the correct green processes are being followed and they will also be responsible for measuring the results. However, it won't do to just have anyone in this position. This job should be filled by someone who is highly familiar with the type of manufacturing that your business already does.

Communicate your progress: A large part of whether or not your green manufacturing works will be due to how well you communicate your progress. This progress should not only be communicated to your employees but your customers, suppliers, and anyone else who is directly involved with your business. You should send out this information in detail and let people know what is being done, how it is being measured, and how close you are to achieving your green manufacturing goals.

One step at a time: Many times manufacturing business owners become so overwhelmed at the idea of green manufacturing that they don't even begin. This is unfortunate. If you fail to move toward green manufacturing you are depriving your business of the benefits that green manufacturing can bring about. If you are a manufacturing business owner it is important to understand that there are many small ways that you can begin to change your manufacturing process and make it green. There is no need to do a complete overhaul if you can only change one process at a time. The bottom line is that every small change you make brings you closer to green manufacturing and the benefits that it provides.

Chapter 6: Tips to Help Manufacturers Go Green

Green manufacturing has moved from being a buzzword in the industry of manufacturing to being a required component. More and more manufacturing companies are seeing the benefits of going green in not just the production process but all throughout their entire company. This turn towards using green manufacturing is not only good for the environment but manufacturing companies that are implementing these measures are finding significant costs savings and huge jumps in customer good will.

If you are the owner of a manufacturing company looking to go green, here are some tips to help you get started.

Do some research: It is crucial that you take the time to educate yourself about green manufacturing principles. This is the best way to determine what green practices will be best for your manufacturing business. Talking to other manufacturing business owners who have made the move to green practices can also give you better insight into how to develop a plan for your company. Do not underestimate the need for sufficient research since this is how you will plan the best green measures that will meet your needs.

Start small: Many manufacturing companies begin with fairly small measures when it comes to green manufacturing. Implementing recycling stations can be a great way to begin with green manufacturing. However, it is important to keep in mind that any green practices that you put in place will require employee training. Management will also need to be heavily supporting the practices in order to get employees enthused and supportive about whatever changes are being made. We recommend that companies make small changes and only a few at a time. Once the changes have taken hold within the company culture then it is time to move on to establishing other green manufacturing practices.

Figure out where you can change: As you implement these smaller green changes such as recycling or using vendors that use only green practices it is time to begin researching where other bigger green changes can be made. It is important to understand that you won't know where you can gain cost savings from implementing green manufacturing until you know where the money is being spent. One of the first steps is to do energy audit. This can help you to better see where your energy is being used and where it will be the most beneficial for your manufacturing company to go green. The energy audit can indentify several key areas where you can save on energy costs both now and in the future.

Look up: One of the biggest energy wasters within many manufacturing companies comes from the ceiling. Both the lights and the heating and cooling systems can be high energy users. Many manufacturing companies have found that by simply replacing their lights with more energy efficient (green) products and putting on timed controls, they can reduce their energy consumption by over 50%. A manufacturing lighting specialist can help you determine where the changes should be made. Another significant energy use for most manufacturing companies comes from the heating and cooling they do within their building. If you are a manufacturing business owner you may be surprised to learn that up to 30% of your energy bill may come from your HVAC system. Simply by having your heating and cooling system looked at and evaluated you can then make changes that will have a significant decrease on the amount that you are spending within your business.

Chapter 7: Implementing Green Manufacturing Beyond the Basics

Green manufacturing has now moved into the forefront of the manufacturing industry. More and more businesses are seeing the benefits of implementing green manufacturing into their overall manufacturing strategy. However, while most companies are familiar with the reuse, renew, recycle aspect of green manufacturing many others do not realize that there are many different aspects of green manufacturing beyond the basics. Adding these additional factors into the overall manufacturing strategy of your business can help you to take "going green" a whole lot further.

Here is what you need to know about implementing green manufacturing beyond the basics

Consider implementing green into what you are already doing: One of the easiest ways to take your green manufacturing initiatives a step further is to work on incorporating green manufacturing into what you are already doing. There are a number of ways to do this especially in your existing sourcing and procurement methods. However, you must be able to keep in mind that this will be a lot more than just considering price. You will need to consider how your procurement and sourcing falls in line with your green manufacturing goals. You will have to find out much more detailed information about the type of methods that your suppliers use. For example: You will need to know what chemicals if any are used in the materials that you are procuring. You should also keep in mind that any of the language that is used either verbal or written should indicate that materials are approved and preferred as to green practices and if possible any raw materials that you procure should be long lasting such as recyclable or rechargeable.

Communicate with your suppliers: In order to move further along with your green manufacturing you will need to have an open line of communication with your suppliers. You will need to set clear expectations especially during your sourcing. You must be vocal about your commitment to sustainability if you expect your suppliers to take your green manufacturing efforts seriously. You will also have to be very proactive about monitoring the compliance that your suppliers have when it comes to green manufacturing. You want to let your suppliers know exactly what they will be expected to provide and how that will be measured. This will help to make sure that the necessary processes are in place to make sure they are being complaint.

Keep up with best practices: One of the most important ways to implement green manufacturing is to stay current with the best practices for your industry. You want to make it a priority to know what the best new materials, technologies, and processes are for the type of manufacturing that your business does. The reason for this is that by staying informed you can better incorporate green manufacturing into your overall manufacturing strategy in the most efficient way possible. You can do this by reading trade publications, participating in groups that are affiliated with your industry, and searching the internet to get the information that you need. This will help you to maintain a competitive advantage and not lose your market share.

Let others know about your progress: Another more immediate way to implement green manufacturing is to take your efforts to the people who matter the most your customers and your employees. When your customers know of your green manufacturing efforts they are far more likely to support your business since this is a major concern for most consumers today.

Finally, letting your employee know what you want to accomplish gets them on board and working with you to accomplish your green manufacturing goals.

Chapter 8: Energy Revolution

The energy revolution is upon us and a number of companies have turned to green manufacturing techniques to save money and improve production. Not only does it help you save money, green manufacturing is a wonderful way to contribute to the energy revolution and focus on protecting the environment.

Environmental issues are starting to catch up with just about every business and almost everyone out there is looking for something they can do to help the energy revolution. Simple things like turning off your air conditioner during peak hours or setting the temperature at a higher rate can help to reduce energy costs. The other thing a number of companies, specifically supermarkets are doing is shutting off half of their lights and switching to energy-efficient bulbs that don't consume as much power.

By doing small things to conserve energy, your manufacturing plant will help to preserve non-renewable sources of energy and it leads to happier customers as many customers are seeking to deal only with companies that are focusing on green manufacturing.

What are some of the common green manufacturing processes you can implement?

Here are the most popular:
1. Utility instruments.

2. Level controllers.
3. Control panels.
4. Process control equipment

Using these different products will help you to conserve energy. Using the different tools in addition to easy energy things like shutting off lights and recycling your excess materials will lead to a green manufacturing environment.

Automation tools are perfect for manufacturing plants. They help to limit the amount of water that is used for flushing toilets along with washing hands and other things. Automation also helps with lights as it will shut off the lights when motion is not detected or it will shut off after a certain amount of time. A lot of the automation tools can help with controlling of appliances at the office like your coffee machines. Having remote access to your system is perfect as it helps you to keep in touch with your plant when you aren't on site and you need to focus on keeping the energy costs down.

By installing automation devices that help to cut your energy costs along with your water and other costs, you will see a 20-80% drop in your energy costs. A number of manufacturing plants are using solar energy to help generate enough energy to sustain the plant. The initial costs will be expensive but they will drop shortly as you see the benefits in turning to solar energy instead of using traditional energy costs.

The energy revolution is helping to reduce the costs of raw goods and other supplies you need in order to run your business. By looking for suppliers that use recycled products, you can save yourself a ton of money. Green products are just about everywhere right now and you won't have a hard time finding them to aid your manufacturing plant.

Look for new equipment that is energy efficient. Older equipment uses more energy, just take a look at the older refrigerators compared to the new ones that use half the energy as the older ones. Check with your suppliers to see if they have new equipment and will trade in your old equipment for a credit on new equipment.

Implement a recycling program within your manufacturing plant as well. While it won't actually save you money on anything, it's a great way to help contribute to the environment. It's also nice to show and tell your customers that you are contributing to the environment and that you have implemented a great recycling program.

Chapter 9: Rooftop Gardens and Solar Plates

Is it for you?

Solar energy is starting to spark more interest among manufacturing plants and other facilities. Should you convert to solar energy? While the costs of installing solar energy are expensive, it can save you more money in the long run as you won't actually have a power bill. However, how can you generate enough energy to power your entire plant? What would happen to the power during a storm? Would you need to switch to alternative power sources during this time?

The use of solar energy has been promoted for a number of years but recently it seems to gain more attention as global warming is a growing concern and many people see pollution issues. Since pollution is controllable, it is important for your manufacturing plant to look for ways to limit the amount of pollution you are creating.

To generate solar energy, you will need to install solar panels. Solar panels are made by a variety of glasses and they will be charged when they are in direct contact with the sun. If you have seen the smaller solar lights for your yard, it is essentially the same type of thing as the glass will "grab" the sunlight's energy all day and will charge atoms and convert them to energy for your manufacturing plant. However you need direct contact with the sunlight in order for it to work.

You will then need a connected inverter which will take the sunlight's energy and convert it to DC electricity and AC electricity. Most businesses will install the solar panels right on top of their roof as this is the best place to get in contact with the sun. Make sure you don't have trees that block the sunlight and you only want to use the solar energy if your plant is far away from other buildings that could cast shadows on the solar panels.

How much money can you expect to save?

Right now customers that use solar energy in their homes see a savings of about 80 to 100 percent on their utility bills. This is because they completely rely on solar energy only to power their home.

Solar panels are starting to drop in price as they are becoming more popular and there is a greater demand for them. One advantage you will also experience with solar panels is the ability to market your manufacturing plant as a green manufacturing plant. Many customers are choosing only to work with companies that have focused on saving energy and reducing the amount of excess waste and other things that are being contributed to the environment.

The other way to earn more attention in your industry is by installing rooftop gardens. Many companies are using rooftop gardens as a way to give their employees a place to "escape" to when they are in need of a break. Rooftop gardens are a nice way to reduce pollution and many plants are actually using the gardens to grow foods to donate to food shelters or to use the foods in their production process. Make sure installing a rooftop garden is a possibility for your company before you just try to do it. There are several different regulations you need to follow with rooftop gardens. They are a lot of fun for your facility, especially if you are in a populated district where your employees don't have a lot of opportunity to go outside and catch some fresh air in a nice garden environment.

Green manufacturing is the future. What are you doing to reduce pollution and to take your manufacturing plant into the new wave of the future?

Chapter 10: Saving the Planet with Green Manufacturing

More companies are taking the initiative to go green and reduce their impact on the environment. Green manufacturing is a great way to gain positive publicity for your company but more than that it's a cost effective way to make sure your employees and your overall company is healthier.

Green manufacturing focuses on limiting your impact on the environment which you can do through smart product development. Can you create products that use less energy? How about setting up a recycling program? Have you tried shutting off lights and turning off equipment in order to use less energy?

Here are some tips you can follow in order to convert your plant to a green manufacturing facility

1. Reduce your consumption of natural resources. Try using solar energy and power to fuel your business.

2. Unplug machines that are not in use. Leaving the machines plugged in actually does suck power despite what you may think. This is why it's also a good idea to turn off your computers at night and to unplug the surge protectors so extra energy is not being wasted.

3. Reduce your emission of toxic chemicals and materials.

4. Reduce the amount of waste your company produces.

5. Change your lights to energy-saving lights.

6. Introduce a recycling program within the company and encourage employees to dump recyclable materials into the correct bins.

7. Start purchasing green products and encourage your employees to do the same.

8. Purchase a water fountain and avoid using bottled water. Encourage employees to use their own bottles to hold the water.

9. Set up a system where lights are motion sensitive and will shut off after 10 minutes of inactivity. This way you will be able to save power by shutting off lights in rooms that are not in use.

10. Purchase green materials like recycled paper and plastics.

By implementing lean manufacturing you can reduce your wasted products and impact on the environment by 70% or more. Green manufacturing is a new approach to the way you do business and it may not always be the easiest thing for your employees to jump on board with. Just make sure everyone understands why you are suddenly changing the way you have been doing business for years. Adopting a green approach to manufacturing will only work if everyone is on board with the new system and has a commitment to improving the environment.

A number of companies that have implemented green manufacturing have been able to reduce costs. Since you are working with recycled materials and you are trying to recycle some of your own materials, you are not producing as much waste.

Here are a few things you can implement in your manufacturing plant to cut costs and go green

Recycled paper: Saving paper is one of the easiest things to do, especially if you operating a printing plant.

Streamlining inventory: Instead of producing products that will sit on the shelves for years make your products to order. This means you will generate a steady workload that is able to keep up with customer demands. Doing so may allow you to reduce waste depending upon what type of business you are in.

Ink: Do you find yourself printing out documents only to throw them away? You can dramatically cut ink costs by bookmarking pages and by using online versions of documents instead of printing them. Switching to black ink from coloured ink can also reduce wasted ink.

Do your best to create products that are earth friendly: This will win over some customers for your business as a lot of people are trying to purchase only from green companies.

Chapter 11: Benefits of Going to Green Manufacturing

Going green is the transformation of moving into a socially and environmentally enterprise that delivers measurable benefits. These benefits can affect the company, the consumer, their communities, and their shareholders.

Going green has become the newest item in the mission statement of several manufacturing companies. The controversy surrounding global warming and manufacturing companies tends to often dominate conversations between environmentalists and manufacturing companies. In order to reduce waste, several manufacturing companies have begun going green.

How do you get to the benefits and what exactly are they? Well look deeper into what is happening in many manufacturing businesses currently. There is plenty of going green changes happening. It is just something that takes a deeper look to see sometimes.

The major benefit to going green is that the changes that occur, can significantly impact the damage that is done on the earth and our environment. Manufacturers that generate increased value through using reduced ways of impacting the environment are going green.

Ways that this can be accomplished is by using machines, tools, and resources that are environmental and earth friendly. Using things like wind turbine development and solar power can not only be much kinder to the environment, but it can also start to save the manufacturers money.

As with all benefits there have been some concerns for safety, ecological ramifications, and local economic impact. Well with this in mind, you know that there are several different outlooks that need to be considered. However even with these few concerns. The measure that needs to be taken for overall safety, outweigh what the costs will come out to. Both for the environment and the manufacturing company themselves.

When you implement going green the overall positive benefits of jobs, environmental health, electricity diversity, and air quality will outweigh most anything that could come up.

It is not only the benefits that are a huge determining factor in the creation of going green for manufacturing companies. But it is also the fact that it is our responsibilities as human beings to care for the earth and atmosphere we live in. If you consider the growth of damage that is currently causing global warming? Then you will see that the changes in the way manufacturing among many other sources need to happen for our safety and the safety of the world.

So above all other benefits, would you not think that having a world around for our children and grandchildren would be enough to get people thinking? That is what needs to be considered. In addition to saved money, more jobs and the pride to know that you care.

Manufacturing equipment is also made to be fast, reliable, and energy efficient. One example of going green is the energy-efficient light bulb. These bulbs use almost half the energy as a standard light bulb and yet they still produce a good amount of light. Manufacturing companies are using this example and re-designing their machines. Going green can benefit your manufacturing company in many ways. Not only will it benefit the environment, but it will impact your consumer, the shareholders, and the company perception in the market.

Another benefit to going green is the impact it will have on the environment. Insurance companies are actually giving better rates to manufacturing companies that are taking steps to go green. The government is even offering tax breaks for manufacturers that have gone green.

Money saving is another benefit to going green. Manufacturers can look for machinery that is earth friendly. Wind and solar energy can save your company thousands of dollars/pounds and it is a very simple way to go green. The reality is that if you can save money on energy, your product costs can go down and your customers will not need to pay as much. In addition you can always maintain the same costs and turn a great profit on your products, helping out your shareholders.

Renewable energy sources are considered to be one of the fastest-growing job markets. New manufacturing plants that are opening with renewable energy sources are offering many more jobs to their communities, giving them a larger respect in their market. Studies show that manufacturing companies that have gone green are expected to employ almost 70 percent of the new jobs in the future; the runner-up is jobs in information technology.

It is important to understand that even though going green has its benefits; it will be a large investment. There are also safety concerns that come with going green, especially if you are re-designing a facility that is currently in use. You may need to shut down parts of the facility while you install new equipment and transform your power source to renewable energy.

Although the costs can be high initially, the benefits will far outweigh them. Both the manufacturing company and the environment will benefit greatly from going green.

It has been shown that employees that work for companies that have gone green highly value the company and they often have a higher performance level than other company's employees. Going green can also produces a better air quality for the employees and the community.

Better air quality may be one of the biggest benefits of going green. With the public awareness surrounding going green, it is also important to go green to keep your manufacturing company competitive. Some customers have begun making purchasing decisions based on products that are manufactured at facilities that have gone green and they boycott the other companies that do not have green manufacturing plants.

The current damage to the earth has many concerned about global warming and the air quality. Going green is not only important for your employees and your community, but can be better for the bottom line.

Chapter 12: How to Take your Manufacturing Business Green

As more people are becoming concerned with our environment and the effects that big and little manufacturing companies are having on the environment, you are going to need to make some changes in how you are going about your business. Currently there are already rules and regulations that you must follow to help with our environment, but more companies are finding that just following those rules is not enough, there clients are wanting safer products because that is what their customers are demanding. Therefore, as a manufacturer you are going to have to decide if going green is right for you.

Here are some things that you are going to need to do in order to make your manufacturing green. Keep in mind that some of these tips might not apply to your manufacturing plant and just because they do not apply to your plant doesn't mean you can't make any changes.

Tip one

One of the first things that you will need to do is to find some alternate means of getting energy for your manufacturing plant. There is plenty of new technology that is available that will allow you to choose different ways of obtaining energy. This doesn't mean that all of your energy has to come from alternative means, but the less amount of traditional energy sources you use the lower your air pollution will be.

Tip two

Another thing that you should do is to find ways that your finished product can be recycled. Many products are currently being recycled today such as old cell phones, ink cartridges, soda cans, paper, etc. The best part is that as time goes on more products are becoming a part of the recycling trend. If you can find a way to recycle or reuse your product you are well on your way to doing, your part in keeping your customers happy and the landfills less crowded. Not only should you look into finding ways to recycle your finished product, but you can also look into recycling any wasted product or excess parts that you might have left over.

Manufacturing products often means that you have damaged products that cannot be sent out to your customers or you have unfinished products that will not be useful for anybody. Going green entails looking into ways to reduce the impact those unneeded parts and products will have on the environment.

Tip three

If you make products that are consumed by other people or are for personal use, you should look into using all natural products. Many products today can be made from natural ingredients for about the same cost. Even if it is, a little more expensive, people are still willing to pay the extra price for products that are free of chemicals. The natural products that you are using can also be used to package your final product, if you need to use packaging at all anymore.

Tip four

A great way to go green is to use recycled products for your packaging. This will help reduce the amount of waste that is in the landfill and can lower your costs because you are not using new materials each time, and everyone knows that recycled products are cheaper to buy than new products.

Tip five

Set up recycle bins throughout your manufacturing plant for your employees to use to recycle everyday items, such as plastic bottles, metal, glass, paper, etc. The little things often make a bigger difference than we are aware of. Recycling needs to be done at all levels of your manufacturing plant in order for it to be successful.

Turning your manufacturing plant into a green manufacturing plant is one of the best ways to keep your clients happy, you don't have to do everything natural even just a few small steps can help save energy and produce less waste and pollution.

Chapter 13: Waste Reduction Manufacturing

Waste reduction seems to be a very simple concept, but there are many different ways to consider it and to start implementing processes that will ensure it works. Waste can be reduced in almost everything we do in our personal lives, but it's also a very important consideration for manufacturing companies and everything they do.

Here is some more information about waste reduction in manufacturing.

The basic belief behind waste reduction for most business is, sadly, less than benevolent and is mostly a consideration for the bottom line of the company. While recent pressure to become green may have increased the desire of companies to waste less, they also want to decrease waste to ensure greater profit margins. If something is sold at the same price but less material, labour and effort is needed to produce it, then this is seen as a gain for the company. While waste minimization for a company often requires an investment of capital and time, it is almost always paid for with increased efficiency and more goodwill towards the company as well.

There are many different processes that can be used to reduce the amount of waste used in any organization or process. One of the most obvious ones is called resource optimization. This involves using raw materials more efficiently to decrease costs and the impact on the environment. One interesting example is the use of fabric and the way that a garment is designed using computers to make the most out of every piece of fabric that goes onto the production line. This is done by having a computer program arrange the various pieces of a pattern in such a way that it gets the maximum amount of use from a small piece of fabric as possible.

Another aspect of resource optimization is the reuse of scrap material. This is only useful in some cases, but the most common use is that of scrap metal. The properties of most metals allow it to be melted and used again for the same purpose. This process can be challenging to implement and can also be costly, but should always be weighed against the alternative of purchasing more material. The decision to reduce the amount of material is almost always a conscious decision and there are numbers behind the idea to back up the actions.

Improving quality control measures can also ensure that less material is wasted and ultimately the end consumer will be more satisfied as well. Process monitoring can quickly alert someone if there is a fault or defect that will compromise the quality of the product or cause it to fail prematurely. Many high tech processes have these kinds of measures in place and they are especially important in the manufacture of consumable goods as well.

Other parts of the process, like product design, can also be improved resulting in lower costs. This may require a significant amount of time to be invested in the process and management of the system before it is actually implemented, but it will help give returns on the investment as the process is carried out. The design of the product and the process that will be used to produce it is very important in making the most of the manufacturing process.

Improving the durability and quality of products can also reduce the amount of waste. Many consumers believe that this method is rarely if ever used because most companies are only interested in the short term profits that will come from producing materials to sell to the public. But, making a product more durable and making it last longer will use less material over time and require that people purchase less of the product or a similar product in the long run. It is rare to find companies with this view, but they are out there and many more are joining the cause to create less waste.

Buying products that include recycled materials and manufacturing your own products with reused materials are great ideas to help improve the quality of life. Through the implementation of the waste reduction programs, companies have been known to save lots of money annually, all for just a small investment in energy and time.

The implementation of a waste reduction program is much easier to achieve with the right direction and support from the top management. Top management should present the idea of waste reduction and recycle programs to its team members and offer meetings and training to further develop the idea. Make sure everyone, including managers, is informed and involved.

Evaluate the location of waste and recycling containers. See that all bins are easily accessible to employees and close to the point of waste. For example, you may notice that an office waste paper bin is next to the fax machine or the printer. Make sure waste and recycling containers are easy to reach and have easy and wide opening to drop recycled materials in. Take the time to check out the condition of the containers. If they are dirty or overflowing, let someone know or take care of the matter yourself by removing or replacing the bins with clean or empty ones.

Continually make your staff members aware of the waste and recycling programs. Posts signs or place waste and recycling containers in plain view of anyone passing by. You can start a program with the idea of reusing packaging and pallets for shipping and receiving. You can work with suppliers to use returnable and reusable containers. You can encourage your staff members to use their own coffee mug instead of the paper cups and you can replace cafeteria paper products with long lasting items. You can think of buying all reusable glassware and silverware supplies including the table linen and serving equipment for company parties or events. You can offer ways to design and manufacture products with reusable parts. You can sell or donate non-functioning equipment to others that can use them.

You need to be informed about the use of toxic chemical materials in your workplace and you should try to replace or change your choice of purchasing toxic chemical materials. Of course, make sure you dispose of the toxic chemical materials properly following all regulations. For your office supplies, order or purchase products only made out of recycled and recyclable materials as well as those that have less toxic chemicals. For all your shipping, use corrugated board packaging that is very easy to recycle.

In general, white paper, corrugated cardboard and aluminium cans are the easiest to recycle. Other recyclable materials can be added as the waste and recycle program continue to grow and are well implemented by your company.

There are so many valid reasons to reduce waste. One of them can be to demonstrate serious concerns for the environment, others can be to help enhance and beautify your outside and inside work area which create a positive public image and increase customer and employee retention. Moreover, reducing waste can improve the overall company's efficiency and profitability.

For a waste reduction program to be successful, it is necessary for the top management to show concern and offer support. The general managers and the executive team members must show their support with their own example. Words are not good enough. Employees watch their leaders to see if they actually participate in the program with actions as well as with words. It is important that everyone is involved and that individuals feel that they can truly make a difference.

Chapter 14: Benefits of Waste Elimination in Manufacturing

There are some serious problems that beset every business, and waste is one of the most severe. A company that reduce wastes is a company that could be doing much better. Waste occurs in many forms; waste can be overproduction, lost time, lost resources, or poor use of raw materials. These are just a few examples of the literally thousands of forms that waste can take.

Many companies are unaware of areas in their business that are wasting valuable time or resources. Although companies are constantly looking for ways to increase their sales, they don't think about cutting waste and streamlining their process. Streamlining is a process through which a company eliminates waste in its production process. This can occur in just about any industry; heavy manufacturing or information technology businesses can undergo streamlining because they can all undergo waste elimination. The benefits of waste elimination cannot be underestimated. Cutting waste means increasing total operating income, which can translate into expanded production capability. A streamlined business is also able to more accurately deliver its products. It avoids the common and serious problem of over production that plagues so many businesses.

Another very real benefit of waste elimination is that you can brag about it. As your company becomes more efficient you can show this to investors. A company that appears to be streamlining its production process is one that appears to be cutting edge and on the up and up. Eliminating waste could easily help to increase stock value or to boost investor confidence.

Take a serious look at your manufacturing business and you will find that there is some sort of waste in almost every area of the company's operation. Even if the waste is minimal, in the long run you will find that your efficiency will improve drastically with minor changes. Imagine a small amount of waste continuing over several years and you can see just how much money and time can be lost. One reason why many businesses allow this type of waste continue is because they are either unaware that it exists, or because they simply don't have the time or energy to deal with the problem. Often managers are overworked and lack the time to make serious changes in their business. They become complacent and let the status quo ride of it makes a profit.

Although everyone is entitled to make their own choices about their business, people have to realize that they won't increase profits very easily without streamlining. And as many more companies find ways to decrease waste you will find that your competitors are starting to get an edge over you. Companies that run efficiently without waste gain positive reputations. Imagine a company like Toyota and the edge it has gained over American car makers. Much of this positive image is the result of waste elimination techniques and streamlining that have produced both better cars and a far cheaper production process.

If you are looking for some method through which to improve your business consider a strategic waste elimination plan. Begin by identifying problem areas and investing in waste saving procedures. This could be a new machine or simply a new way of doing things. Be creative and realize that waste comes in many forms. Don't be afraid to change things drastically; sometimes a business needs dramatic change before it can get to where it wants to be. With some patience, hard work, and waste elimination you will be able to grow your business and improve its image. Good luck eliminating the waste that holds your business back.

Chapter 15: Waste Management Options

With manufacturing comes waste. However, when dealing with the excess of your particular trade there are options available for reducing the amount of waste produced and or dealing with the surplus. Simple waste management techniques can help your business save money as well. Below are a few tips and suggestions to help in reducing and managing your leftover materials.

The first step in reducing or managing any kind of program is participation. This isn't referring to employee participation so much as executive participation. The program has to be led from the top down for success to follow. If employees see that the top level executives participate and strongly follow the guidelines then they themselves are more willing to do so. The plan needs to be implemented from the top down. Words won't cut it. Everyone has to get involved and feel as if their part in the program helps to make a difference.

Tip 1

Look at what materials you currently are consuming and how much of it you then dispose of. Do some analysis to see if there are any additional uses for that material. Are there ways in which to retool the processes to utilize more of material? Ask for suggestions from your employees. The ones that deal with the material regularly may see something that you don't as an executive.

Tip 2

Shop around. Look at what you currently use for materials and see if there are other goods that can be used that are recycled themselves or more suitable to recycling. Remember that you don't want to lose quality grades and that costs might increase some. However, over the long run you may end up saving in other areas (disposal fees, etc). Be informed about the types of toxic wastes you are using. See if there aren't substitutes available. Make sure you dispose of any toxic wastes according to guidelines established for the well being of all.

Tip 3

Change your shipping materials. Use corrugated cardboard instead of other materials. Corrugated cardboard can be easily recycled.

Tip 4

Provide waste recycling bins. Carefully evaluate where they are placed. Make sure that the bins are easily accessible and close to the points of waste. For example, a bin placed next to a printer in an office. Most individuals will not go out of their way to make sure excess is being disposed of properly. Bins should be available with wide openings for ease of access. Don't make the process complicated. Make sure they are easily identifiable and labelled. If an employee can't tell easily what's supposed to go inside of the bin, they won't use it.

Tip 5

Make sure the bins are managed with care. Maybe you make it someone's specific duty to manage and care for the bins. If they are full empty them, if they are dirty or overly used, replace them and clean them up. If your employees see that the bins are being taken care of and that it is making a difference they will continue to use them with confidence.

Tip 6

Make sure your recycling and waste management programs are made known to employees. Don't just send out a memo and hope everyone reads it. Place signs and placards in high traffic places. Make it a part of training or staff meetings. Most importantly lead by example.

Tip 7

Check and work with suppliers to see if you can use returnable and reusable materials for transport, etc. Simple things like reusing pallets can save lots of money and trees.

Tip 8

Eliminate the disposable paper products used in offices and break rooms. Encourage individuals to bring their own mugs, silver ware, etc. Provide access to a sink and dish soap. For company parties and events change out the paper linens for real ones. Use glassware and silver ware. It may take a little more effort in the clean up, but the savings will be worth it in the long run.

Tip 9

Donate or sell unused or non-functioning equipment. Maybe another company has the ability to fix a machine that you no longer need.

Chapter 16: Encouraging Recycling at your Manufacturing Plant

Several manufacturing companies do not properly dispose of their waste, causing thousands of dollars/pounds to be lost. There are numerous reasons why recycling should be encouraged at your manufacturing plant. Not only is it beneficial for the environment, but it also saves your company money. Recycling plants often will contract with manufacturing companies to pick up their waste materials that can be recycled.

If you do not have a recycling program already in place, here are a few tips to encourage recycling at your manufacturing plant.

Tip 1: Decide what products can be recycled.

One of the easiest ways to start recycling is to look at all the products that can be recycled. Paper, plastic, and metals can all be recycled. Look at all the items that are currently being tossed into the trash. Can any of these items be recycled? Can some of these items be used for other purposes at the facility? Find out what items can be re-used and hang onto them. Only save the materials that will benefit your company. Hanging onto a large wooden box won't do you much good if your company manufacturers metal or plastic.

Tip 2: Establish recycling rules at your plant.

The next thing you need to do is tell everyone at your plant about your new recycling program. Make sure they understand what materials can be recycled and where they need to place these items. Place large recycling bins around the workplace and encourage your staff members to use them. If you place smaller recycling bins in the same area as the trash cans, employees will remember to use them. Label the recycling bins so employees know what materials can be placed in them. For example, you can have 3 separate bins all marked with a different thing like "plastic", "paper", or "metal." The recycling bins only work if employees know where they are located. Picking central locations or placing them next to garbage cans will eliminate a lot of confusion.

Tip 3: Hold training meetings.

After you install the new recycling bins, pay attention to how they are being used. After about 2 weeks, hold another training meeting to tell your employees about the importance of recycling. If you notice your employees are still using the garbage cans, remove most of them from the facility. Only have one garbage can in the facility, this will encourage staff members to recycle because they have to walk further to find a trash can. If your employees still aren't catching onto the recycling program, bring in some recycling specialists to talk to them about recycling.

During the meeting, talk to your employees about the impact recycling has on the environment. The recycling specialist can talk to your employees about the benefits of recycling and the effects it has on them at an individual level. When people identify with a cause, they are willing to fix the problem.

Involve your employees in the recycling process by having them come up with some creative recycling ideas. Make the entire experience is fun for everyone involved and not just another assignment that they have to do. A simple way to encourage recycling at your facility is to use a reward chart. Employees that are caught making efforts to recycle on a continual basis will be rewarded. The reward doesn't have to be something big, just something simple enough to get their attention and to show them they are appreciated. People love to get free stuff and they will make efforts toward recycling if they know there is a chance of getting something for free. Over time recycling will become a habit and everyone at your facility will be involved.

It seems as if there are far too many businesses that do not take advantage of recycling their materials. Studies have been done, and found that a lot of material is being dumped was waste, rather than re-used as a resource. So how do you encourage recycling at your manufacturing plant? Each day manufacturing companies throw out valuable trash. Materials that are commonly generated in the manufacturing industry such as paper, plastics, and metals can all be recycled and recovered. Here are some tips on how to encourage recycling at your manufacturing plant.

The first thing you can do if it has not been done already is to start recycling at your manufacturing plant and establish a waste reduction and recycling program. Take a good look around the plant, and have employees to do the same. What is being thrown away? Can anything be salvaged and used somewhere else? Can anything be separated for recycling? Find the target materials and figure out where they can be used. Target materials that are specific to your company. For example, one type of manufacturing may have different recycling material than another.

The best way to manage your waste is to not create any, so consider these things as you try to encourage recycling in your manufacturing plant.

Use non-hazardous materials instead of hazardous. Don't mix more of something than you will need. You can always go back for more. Reuse parts of your old equipment before purchasing new parts. Encourage your employees to come up with creative ways to dispose of their own waste.

Chapter 17: What are the Real Costs of Going Green

Passionate is the debate about the manufacturing's efforts and abilities to "go green." Politicians are quick to assign the government with the responsibility to assign funds to those manufacturers who are willing to transition their plants into organizations more conscious of environmental effects and preservation. It is where the money is to come from to sponsor the greening of the manufacturing industry that becomes the real issue. One US politician has pushed for what she called the creation of a Strategic Energy Fund. The Strategic Energy Fund would create "green collar" jobs in the manufacturing industry, thus boosting low employment rates and improving energy efficient technology. This fund is proposed to be funded by a tax on oil companies, however with the proposed total contribution of the fund at about $50 billion, you can bet that oil companies are not going to be thrilled with such a proposal.

The question of turning a company green is really a matter of money. The only reason why a manufacturing plant would resist the implementation of green technology is because of the costs that are associated with recreating the manufacturing process of an entire manufacturing plant. In some respects it is like starting the company over from scratch. With the government already forcing manufacturing industries to comply with more environmentally friendly standards, the financial stress to go above and beyond government legislation is just too high. Take the US Clean Air Act for example. The Clean Air Act forced many already struggling manufacturing companies to make expensive changes.

So what are the real costs of going green?

Well for many manufacturing plants it is a choice between being more environmentally responsible and allowing employees to keep their jobs. Many companies cannot afford to do both. No reasonable business person would disagree that it is advantageous to keep the air clean and the environment healthy. Yet in terms of dollars and cents it is not easy as environmental advocates would like people to believe.

The petroleum debate is an excellent example that proponents of green living use to illustrate why it pays to go green when you run a manufacturing plant. One side of the argument claims that costs can be reduced on buying fuel from abroad if we are able to supply the needs of our country within our own borders. Also the craze for fuel derived from corn seems like a very popular and sensible way to conserve energy and personal fuel costs. There is always another side of the argument. And, unfortunately, according to recent research the process used to make the PHA, or corn derived fuel for the manufacturing of plastics, consumes nineteen times more electricity, twenty two percent more steam, and seven times more water than the traditional chemical method of manufacturing.

Of course the battle for energy efficiency and production that is not harmful to the environment will continue. Processes of going green have definitely come a long way and many are excited about the possibilities that exist for future generations of manufacturers. Ultimately it pays to go green when you run a manufacturing plant today because of the positive feedback received from environmentally conscious consumers and the increase in awareness and sales because of it. And as processes of green production become more streamline and research and development dollars can be applied elsewhere, a totally green manufacturing plant will benefit from renewable and reusable resources and the cost savings therein. Future financial rewards offer incentives to make significant investments towards going green today.

Chapter 18: Manager's Guide for Going Green

Depending on what type of business you are will depend on what things are important to you. If you want to save money there are some things that you can do. One thing that could be really beneficial to your company is to go green. If you have never heard of going green or want more information on going green you are in luck.

Here is a manager's guide for going green.

Going green is a process where you start using more eco-friendly products that help reduce or eliminate waste and harmful discharges. This can be done in numerous of ways.

Find out what harmful wastes and emissions are you using in your industry. You will want to make sure that you pinpoint what your company is doing that damages the planet and then try to change it. There are a lot of things that you can do to help go green and it won't even cost you that much money.

Make sure that you go green and not just greenish! If you are not going green you cannot ensure that your products have an eco benefit. You can do this for example if in your industry you have containers that you use to fill with certain things. Make your containers reuse able. This will not only help you save money because you won't be constantly buying new ones but it also helps the earth because you are saving energy.

Make sure that you make your goal not only to save financially but also to save the planet. You will want to make sure that when you are coming up with different ideas for making your company go green that you take everything into consideration. Make sure that you make realistic goals that can be met and that it will benefit you and your customers.

Stick to what you are teaching other people. If you are advertising going green and telling everyone else that they should go green you better make sure that you are also going green. The worst publicity you can get is to preach one thing but do another. If people see that you are saying one thing but doing another they will not trust you and in return you might lose customers because of it.

Make sure that you consider the whole picture. Something might cost more up front to make your company go green but over time it might end up saving you a lot of money. You will want to make sure to take these kinds of things into consideration.

These are just some of the things to know as a manager's guide for going green. There are a lot of other things that you could add. You can do different research and read different reviews that pertain to your company that will help you to determine different things that can help you go green. The more you know about going green the better off you will be.

Part 2: Paradigm Shift to Sustainable Capitalism

Chapter 19: Achieving Sustainability

Achieving sustainability will enable the earth to continue supporting human life as we know it.

Sustainability in a general sense is the capacity to support, maintain or endure. Since the 1980s human sustainability has been related to the integration of environmental, economic, and social dimensions towards global stewardship and responsible management of resources. In ecology, sustainability describes how biological systems remain diverse, robust and productive over time, a necessary precondition for the well-being of humans and other organisms.

Sustainable ecosystems and environments provide vital resources and processes (known as "ecosystem services"). There are two major ways of managing human impact on ecosystem services. One approach is environmental management; this approach is based largely on information gained from educated professionals in earth science, environmental science, and conservation biology. Another approach is management of consumption of resources, which is based largely on information gained from educated professionals in economics.

Human sustainability interfaces with economics through the voluntary trade consequences of economic activity. Moving towards sustainability (or applied sustainability) while keeping the quality of life high is a social challenge that entails, among other factors, international and national law, urban planning and transport, local and individual lifestyles and ethical consumerism. Ways of living more sustainably can take many forms from controlling living conditions (e.g., eco-villages, eco-municipalities and sustainable cities), to reappraising work practices (e.g., using perm culture, green building, sustainable agriculture), or developing and using new technologies that reduce the consumption of resources such as renewable energy technologies.

At the 2005 World Summit on Social Development it was noted that this requires the reconciliation of environmental, social equity and economic demands the "three pillars" of sustainability or (the 3 Es). This view has been expressed as an illustration using three overlapping ellipses indicating that the three pillars of sustainability are not mutually exclusive and can be mutually reinforcing. The three pillars have served as a common ground for numerous sustainability standards and certification systems in recent years, in particular in the food industry. Standards which today explicitly refer to the triple bottom line include Rainforest Alliance, Fair-trade and UTZ Certified. The triple bottom line is also recognized by the ISEAL Alliance; the global association for social and environmental standards.

Sustainable development as defined by the UN is not universally accepted and has undergone various interpretations. What sustainability is, what its goals should be, and how these goals are to be achieved are all open to interpretation. For many environmentalists 'sustainable development' is an oxymoron as development seems to entail environmental degradation. Ecological economist Herman Daly has asked, "what use is a sawmill without a forest?" From this perspective, the economy is a subsystem of human society, which is itself a subsystem of the biosphere and a gain in one sector is a loss from another.

A universally accepted definition of sustainability remains elusive because it needs to be factual and scientific, a clear statement of a specific "destination". The simple definition "sustainability is improving the quality of human life while living within the carrying capacity of supporting eco-systems", though vague, conveys the idea of sustainability having quantifiable limits. But sustainability is also a call to action, a task in progress or "journey" and therefore a political process, so some definitions set out common goals and values. The Earth Charter speaks of "a sustainable global society founded on respect for nature, universal human rights, economic justice, and a culture of peace."

To add complication, the word sustainability is applied not only to human sustainability on Earth, but to many situations and contexts over many scales of space and time, from small local ones to the global balance of production and consumption. It implies responsible and proactive decision-making and innovation that minimizes negative impact and maintains balance between social, environmental, and economic growth to ensure a desirable planet for all species now and in the future. It can also just refer to a future intention: "sustainable agriculture" is not necessarily a current situation but a goal for the future, a prediction. For all these reasons sustainability is perceived, at one extreme, as nothing more than a feel-good buzzword with little meaning or substance but, at the other, as an important but unfocused concept like "liberty" or "justice". It has also been described as a "dialogue of values that defies consensual definition".

Chapter 20: Management of Human Consumption

The underlying driver of direct human impacts on the environment is human consumption. This impact is reduced by not only consuming less but by also making the full cycle of production, use and disposal more sustainable. Consumption of goods and services can be analysed and managed at all scales through the chain of consumption, starting with the effects of individual lifestyle choices and spending patterns, through to the resource demands of specific goods and services, the impacts of economic sectors, through national economies to the global economy. Analysis of consumption patterns relates resource use to the environmental, social and economic impacts at the scale or context under investigation. The ideas of embodied resource use (the total resources needed to produce a product or service), resource intensity, and resource productivity are important tools for understanding the impacts of consumption. Key resource categories relating to human needs are food, energy, materials and water.

In 2010, the International Resource Panel, hosted by the United Nations Environment Programme (UNEP), published the first global scientific assessment on the impacts of consumption and production and identified priority actions for developed and developing countries. The study found that the most critical impacts are related to ecosystem health, human health and resource depletion. From a production perspective, it found that fossil-fuel combusting processes, agriculture and fisheries have the most important impacts. Meanwhile, from a final consumption perspective, it found that household consumption related to mobility, shelter, food and energy-using products cause the majority of life-cycle impacts of consumption.

Energy

The Sun's energy, stored by plants (primary producers) during photosynthesis, passes through the food chain to other organisms to ultimately power all living processes. Since the industrial revolution the concentrated energy of the Sun stored in fossilized plants as fossil fuels has been a major driver of technology which, in turn, has been the source of both economic and political power. In 2007 climate scientists of the IPCC concluded that there was at least a 90% probability that atmospheric increase in CO_2 was human-induced, mostly as a result of fossil fuel emissions but, to a lesser extent from changes in land use. Stabilizing the world's climate will require high-income countries to reduce their emissions by 60–90% over 2006 levels by 2050 which should hold CO_2 levels at 450–650 ppm from current levels of about 380 ppm. Above this level, temperatures could rise by more than 2°C to produce "catastrophic" climate change. Reduction of current CO_2 levels must be achieved against a background of global population increase and developing countries aspiring to energy-intensive high consumption Western lifestyles.

Reducing greenhouse emissions, is being tackled at all scales, ranging from tracking the passage of carbon through the carbon cycle to the commercialization of renewable energy, developing less carbon-hungry technology and transport systems and attempts by individuals to lead carbon neutral lifestyles by monitoring the fossil fuel use embodied in all the goods and services they use.

Water

Water security and food security are inextricably linked. In the decade 1951–60 human water withdrawals were four times greater than the previous decade. This rapid increase resulted from scientific and technological developments impacting through the economy especially the increase in irrigated land, growth in industrial and power sectors, and intensive dam construction on all continents. This altered the water cycle of rivers and lakes, affected their water quality and had a significant impact on the global water cycle. Currently towards 35% of human water use is unsustainable, drawing on diminishing aquifers and reducing the flows of major rivers; this percentage is likely to increase if climate change impacts become more severe, populations increase, aquifers become progressively depleted and supplies become polluted and unsanitary. From 1961 to 2001 water demand doubled; agricultural use increased by 75%, industrial use by more than 200%, and domestic use more than 400%. In the 1990s it was estimated that humans were using 40–50% of the globally available freshwater in the approximate proportion of 70% for agriculture, 22% for industry, and 8% for domestic purposes with total use progressively increasing.

Water efficiency is being improved on a global scale by increased demand management, improved infrastructure, improved water productivity of agriculture, minimising the water intensity (embodied water) of goods and services, addressing shortages in the non-industrialised world, concentrating food production in areas of high productivity, and planning for climate change. At the local level, people are becoming more self-sufficient by harvesting rainwater and reducing use of mains water.

Food

The American Public Health Association (APHA) defines a "sustainable food system" as "one that provides healthy food to meet current food needs while maintaining healthy ecosystems that can also provide food for generations to come with minimal negative impact to the environment. A sustainable food system also encourages local production and distribution infrastructures and makes nutritious food available, accessible, and affordable to all. Further, it is humane and just, protecting farmers and other workers, consumers, and communities." Concerns about the environmental impacts of agribusiness and the stark contrast between the obesity problems of the Western world and the poverty and food insecurity of the developing world have generated a strong movement towards healthy, sustainable eating as a major component of overall ethical consumerism. The environmental effects of different dietary patterns depend on many factors, including the proportion of animal and plant foods consumed and the method of food production.

The World Health Organization has published a Global Strategy on Diet, Physical Activity and Health report which was endorsed by the May 2004 World Health Assembly. It recommends the Mediterranean diet which is associated with health and longevity and is low in meat, rich in fruits and vegetables, low in added sugar and limited salt, and low in saturated fatty acids; the traditional source of fat in the Mediterranean is olive oil, rich in monounsaturated fat. The healthy rice-based Japanese diet is also high in carbohydrates and low in fat. Both diets are low in meat and saturated fats and high in legumes and other vegetables; they are associated with a low incidence of ailments and low environmental impact.

At the global level the environmental impact of agribusiness is being addressed through sustainable agriculture and organic farming. At the local level there are various movements working towards local food production, more productive use of urban wastelands and domestic gardens including urban horticulture, local food, slow food, sustainable gardening, and organic gardening.

Sustainable seafood is seafood from either fished or farmed sources that can maintain or increase production in the future without jeopardizing the ecosystems from which it was acquired. The sustainable seafood movement has gained momentum as more people become aware about both overfishing and environmentally destructive fishing methods.

Materials, toxic substances, waste

An electric wire reel reused as a centre table in a Rio de Janeiro decoration fair. The reuse of materials is a sustainable practice that is rapidly growing among designers in Brazil.

As global population and affluence has increased, so has the use of various materials increased in volume, diversity and distance transported. Included here are raw materials, minerals, synthetic chemicals (including hazardous substances), manufactured products, food, living organisms and waste. By 2050, humanity could consume an estimated 140 billion tons of minerals, ores, fossil fuels and biomass per year (three times its current amount) unless the economic growth rate is decoupled from the rate of natural resource consumption. Developed countries' citizens consume an average of 16 tons of those four key resources per capita (ranging up to 40 or more tons per person in some developed countries with resource consumption levels far beyond what is likely sustainable.

Sustainable use of materials has targeted the idea of dematerialization, converting the linear path of materials (extraction, use, disposal in landfill) to a circular material flow that reuses materials as much as possible, much like the cycling and reuse of waste in nature. This approach is supported by product stewardship and the increasing use of material flow analysis at all levels, especially individual countries and the global economy. The use of sustainable biomaterials that come from renewable sources and that can be recycled is preferred to the use on non-renewable from a life cycle standpoint.

Synthetic chemical production has escalated following the stimulus it received during the Second World War Chemical production includes everything from herbicides, pesticides and fertilizers to domestic chemicals and hazardous substances. Apart from the build-up of greenhouse gas emissions in the atmosphere, chemicals of particular concern include: heavy metals, nuclear waste, chlorofluorocarbons, persistent organic pollutants and all harmful chemicals capable of bioaccumulation. Although most synthetic chemicals are harmless there needs to be rigorous testing of new chemicals, in all countries, for adverse environmental and health effects. International legislation has been established to deal with the global distribution and management of dangerous goods.

Every economic activity produces material that can be classified as waste. To reduce waste industry, business and government are now mimicking nature by turning the waste produced by industrial metabolism into resource. Dematerialization is being encouraged through the ideas of industrial ecology, eco-design and eco-labelling. In addition to the well-established "reduce, reuse and recycle," shoppers are using their purchasing power for ethical consumerism.

Chapter 21: Green Economy

On one account, sustainability "concerns the specification of a set of actions to be taken by present persons that will not diminish the prospects of future persons to enjoy levels of consumption, wealth, utility, or welfare comparable to those enjoyed by present persons."Sustainability interfaces with economics through the social and ecological consequences of economic activity. Sustainability economics represents" a broad interpretation of ecological economics where environmental and ecological variables and issues are basic but part of a multidimensional perspective.

Social, cultural, health-related and monetary/financial aspects have to be integrated into the analysis." However, the concept of sustainability is much broader than the concepts of sustained yield of welfare, resources, or profit margins. At present, the average per capita consumption of people in the developing world is sustainable but population numbers are increasing and individuals are aspiring to high-consumption Western lifestyles. The developed world population is only increasing slightly but consumption levels are unsustainable. The challenge for sustainability is to curb and manage Western consumption while raising the standard of living of the developing world without increasing its resource use and environmental impact. This must be done by using strategies and technology that break the link between, on the one hand, economic growth and on the other, environmental damage and resource depletion.

A recent UNEP report proposes a green economy defined as one that "improves human well-being and social equity, while significantly reducing environmental risks and ecological scarcities": it "does not favour one political perspective over another but works to minimise excessive depletion of natural capital". The report makes three key findings: "that greening not only generates increases in wealth, in particular a gain in ecological commons or natural capital, but also (over a period of six years) produces a higher rate of GDP growth"; that there is "an inextricable link between poverty eradication and better maintenance and conservation of the ecological commons, arising from the benefit flows from natural capital that are received directly by the poor"; "in the transition to a green economy, new jobs are created, which in time exceed the losses in "brown economy" jobs. However, there is a period of job losses in transition, which requires investment in re-skilling and re-educating the workforce".

Several key areas have been targeted for economic analysis and reform; the environmental effects of unconstrained economic growth; the consequences of nature being treated as an economic externality; and the possibility of an economics that takes greater account of the social and environmental consequences of market behaviour.

Historically there has been a close correlation between economic growth and environmental degradation; as communities grow, so the environment declines. Unsustainable economic growth has been starkly compared to the malignant growth of a cancer because it eats away at the Earth's ecosystem services which are its life-support system. There is concern that, unless resource use is checked, modern global civilization will follow the path of ancient civilizations that collapsed through overexploitation of their resource base. While conventional economics is concerned largely with economic growth and the efficient allocation of resources, ecological economics has the explicit goal of sustainable scale (rather than continual growth), fair distribution and efficient allocation, in that order. The World Business Council for Sustainable Development states that "business cannot succeed in societies that fail".

In economic and environmental fields, the term decoupling is becoming increasingly used in the context of economic production and environmental quality. When used in this way, it refers to the ability of an economy to grow without incurring corresponding increases in environmental pressure. Ecological economics includes the study of societal metabolism, the throughput of resources that enter and exit the economic system in relation to environmental quality. An economy that is able to sustain GDP growth without having a negative impact on the environment is said to be decoupled. Exactly how, if, or to what extent this can be achieved is a subject of much debate. In 2011 the International Resource Panel, hosted by the United Nations Environment Programme (UNEP), warned that by

2050 the human race could be devouring 140 billion tons of minerals, ores, fossil fuels and biomass per year; three times its current rate of consumption unless nations can make serious attempts at decoupling.

There are conflicting views whether improvements in technological efficiency and innovation will enable a complete decoupling of economic growth from environmental degradation. On the one hand, it has been claimed repeatedly by efficiency experts that resource use intensity (i.e., energy and materials use per unit GDP) could in principle be reduced by at least four or five-fold, thereby allowing for continued economic growth without increasing resource depletion and associated pollution. On the other hand, an extensive historical analysis of technological efficiency improvements has conclusively shown that energy and materials use efficiency improvements were almost always outpaced by economic growth, in large part because of the rebound effect (conservation).

Chapter 22: Nature as an Economic Externality

The economic importance of nature is indicated by the use of the expression ecosystem services to highlight the market relevance of an increasingly scarce natural world that can no longer be regarded as both unlimited and free. In general, as a commodity or service becomes more scarce the price increases and this acts as a restraint that encourages frugality, technical innovation and alternative products. However, this only applies when the product or service falls within the market system. As ecosystem services are generally treated as economic externalities they are unprized and therefore overused and degraded, a situation sometimes referred to as the Tragedy of the Commons.

One approach to this dilemma has been the attempt to "internalise" these "externalities" by using market strategies like eco-taxes and incentives, trade-able permits for carbon, and the encouragement of payment for ecosystem services.

Economic opportunity

Treating the environment as an externality may generate short-term profit at the expense of sustainability. Sustainable business practices, on the other hand, integrate ecological concerns with social and economic ones (i.e., the triple bottom line).

Growth that depletes ecosystem services is sometimes termed "uneconomic growth" as it leads to a decline in quality of life. Minimising such growth can provide opportunities for local businesses. For example, industrial waste can be treated as an "economic resource in the wrong place". The benefits of waste reduction include savings from disposal costs, fewer environmental penalties, and reduced liability insurance. This may lead to increased market share due to an improved public image. Energy efficiency can also increase profits by reducing costs.

The idea of sustainability as a business opportunity has led to the formation of organizations such as the Sustainability Consortium of the Society for Organizational Learning, the Sustainable Business Institute, and the World Council for Sustainable Development. Research focusing on progressive corporate leaders who have embedded sustainability into commercial strategy has yielded a leadership competency model for sustainability. The expansion of sustainable business opportunities can contribute to job creation through the introduction of green-collar workers.

Social dimension

Sustainability issues are generally expressed in scientific and environmental terms, as well as in ethical terms of stewardship, but implementing change is a social challenge that entails, among other things, international and national law, urban planning and transport, local and individual lifestyles and ethical consumerism. "The relationship between human rights and human development, corporate power and environmental justice, global poverty and citizen action, suggest that responsible global citizenship is an inescapable element of what may at first glance seem to be simply matters of personal consumer and moral choice."

Chapter 23: Green Manufacturing and Resiliency

This chapter is on resiliency and how it relates to manufacturing and, in particular, green and sustainable manufacturing.

In a discussion about leveraging with some experts recently it was suggested that, in fact, leveraging works in both directions; from manufacturing towards the product and from manufacturing back to material selection. We did discuss the "forward" direction with respect to changes in the manufacturing process that may require some investment of resources (or energy, materials, etc.) but which will yield a substantially larger reduction in life cycle impact of the product in use and, hence, a good return on the investment.

We also agreed that the "backward" look is equally sensible but here, we can make decisions in the product design or manufacturing that influences material selection. For example, we can choose to use a production technology that is, perhaps, more energy intensive but allows us to choose from a wider range of materials including some that are less energy intensive to produce (lower embedded energy), less hazardous or better for operation of the product to reduce impact.

That is, we can mirror leveraging in both directions about the manufacturing process. And, interestingly, this could make our systems more reliable and resistant to disruption due to, say, materials shortages or other disruptions due to impacts.

This is a great lead in to our topic in this chapter – resiliency.

The dictionary defines resiliency as "the capability of a strained body to recover its size and shape after deformation caused especially by compressive stress or an ability to recover from or adjust easily to misfortune or change" (and it give the example of "emotional resiliency"). The second definition is probably closest to what interests us here; recovering from unexpected or unwanted change or misfortune. Think supply chain disruption due to, for example, floods in Thailand or earthquakes in Japan.

Actually, we can characterize these disruptions in terms of our ability to foresee or predict the disruption or plan for it. Things like earthquakes are unpredictable. You can choose not to build your factory in an earthquake zone (but some choose not to worry about that if you can build the structure "resiliently"). You can't always predict or anticipate other system stressors like labour disruptions, mineral or material shortages, equipment malfunction, etc. But you can try to take steps to reduce the impact (or inoculate your system from their effects). Planning, redundancy, alternate sources, careful choice of components/suppliers/sources, etc. all can help.

If you Google the term "manufacturing resiliency" you will get a number of postings and articles dealing with reducing downtime due to disasters and other unanticipated events that result in reduced employee productivity, revenue loss, damaged corporate reputation and missed service levels. These "unanticipated events" can be caused by power outages, natural disasters, or other disruptions to manufacturers' supply chains and critical material or part suppliers.

Of course, many suggest that IT is the solution … more information faster means fewer surprises. Maybe.

Resilience was originally introduced by Holling (1973) as a concept to help understand the capacity of ecosystems with alternative attractors to persist in the original state subject to perturbations. In some fields the term resilience has been technically used in a narrow sense to refer to the return rate to equilibrium upon a perturbation (called engineering resilience by Holling in 1996)."

Hollings wrote a foundational paper on resiliency (the full cite is Holling, CS (1973) Resilience and Stability of Ecological Systems, Annual Review of Ecology and Systematics, 4:1–23.) In this paper Hollings discussed the difference between engineering resilience and ecological resilience. He considered that the engineering system has one equilibrium state only, while the ecological system has more than one equilibrium state.

So, simply put, resiliency is the ability of a system (say a supply chain or production system) to return to a stable operable state in the presence of "attractors" (or in engineering terms, disruptions) that would tend to move the system into another state of operation presumably less stable, or less profitable, or less environmentally benign.

It is not too hard to see where risk comes into this and, if the risk is induced by unexpected events (like floods) the resilience of the system will be the ability of the system to return to normalcy with the least disruption. And, with respect to "equilibrium states" it is clear that manufacturing systems may have many (since they have many different components) and it might be preferable to move to a new equilibrium state if it can be shown that it is more green or sustainable!

So, let's draw the conversation back to manufacturing. Equilibrium is a very well understood engineering term and refers to a state of rest or a natural condition that a system will revert to when left alone. In the case of manufacturing, say a production system, equilibrium might be when the system is operating as designed with the requisite result or output. A complex supply chain might be said to be at equilibrium not when it is stopped or doing nothing (as in the engineering definition "state of rest") but when it is functioning smoothly. I realize this is not a precise definition but it will suffice for our discussion of resilience here.

I recently was exposed to the use of resilience with respect to green manufacturing and sustainability in the context of the National Institute of Standards

(NIST) use of the term as part of a description of their sustainable manufacturing program. The site explains that "the sustainable manufacturing program will enable advanced manufacturing processes that include new manufacturing methodologies, manufacturing information systems, and effective industry standards. The Program results will advance U.S. leadership in sustainable manufacturing, resulting in technologies that support the application of Key Performance Indicators (KPI's) to access and decide on production networks which require much less energy and materials, reduced waste and optimal logistics. By using these technologies industries are ideally positioned to optimize their processes and maximize their efficiency and resilience." Lots there; methodologies/technologies, information systems, key performance indicators (KPI's), standards all with the purpose of helping to make decisions on production processes and networks that use less energy and materials, reduced waste and optimal logistics. And, hence, make the processes and networks more resilient!

Chapter 24: Axes of Resiliency as Relating to Green Manufacturing

Response, recovery, regeneration

We continue here our discussion on "resiliency" and how it relates to green and sustainable manufacturing. Recall that I started with a standard dictionary definition of resiliency as the capability of a body under strain to recover its original size and shape after some external disturbance or deformation. It also listed the ability to recover from or "adjust to misfortune or change."

Engineers think of the first definition in terms of a "rubber band" which can be stretched and then, when released, returns to its original shape. This is certainly a recovery from change as well. I also believe this includes "inoculation" to disruption and risk the rubber band is designed to recover.

In the last chapter we ventured into the muddy waters of "equilibrium state" of a manufacturing process or system. The idea was that resilience refers to the ability of an engineering system to return to equilibrium. But, I don't want to confuse equilibrium in the sense of mechanical equilibrium we learned in our early physics course at school. There we said that equilibrium was the state in which the sum of the forces, and torque, on each particle or element of the system is zero or thermal equilibrium wherein there is no exchange of energy between an object and the surrounds meaning everything is at the same temperature.

I inferred that, here, equilibrium was essentially a stable operable state that the system returns to following a disruption that would tend to move the system into another state of operation presumably less stable, or less profitable, or less environmentally benign.

So, what are the various dimensions (or axes) of resiliency?

We can think about measures of responsiveness, recovery and regeneration for starters. Returning to the information from NIST on resilience (specifically National Institute of Standards and Technology, 2008, "Strategic Plan for the National Earthquake Hazards Reduction Program: Fiscal Years 2009-2013") one might argue that resilience entails three interrelated dimensions; reduced failure probabilities; reduced negative consequences when failure does occur; and reduced time required to recover.

So, how do these relate to green or sustainable manufacturing? To what extent can elements of manufacturing, as practiced, be implemented to reduce the likelihood of failure, minimize negative consequences when some disruption or failure occurs and, finally, minimize the time to recover (that is, get back to "equilibrium")?

These are normally topics covered in more conventional manufacturing business practices and system management; mean time to failure and mean time to repair, redundancy, etc.

Chapter 25: Social Impacts in Sustainability

At the end of the last chapter, I was starting to make a connection between resiliency and some of the societal dimensions of sustainability. As we start looking into some of the less technical aspects, like consumer response/acceptance, we get into these more esoteric aspects of green and sustainable manufacturing.

To the extent that larger civil systems are involved in manufacturing supply chains or labour responsiveness, enhancing manufacturing resilience to disruptions and disasters is not a purely technical problem, but involves societal dimensions.

I was reading Fortune magazine few months ago and I noticed an article under a discussion on "What will the Global 500 look like in 2021" (the Global 500 are the top 500 companies internationally.) The article stated that "scarcity will be the new normal" and claimed that "three billion new people will join the global middle class in the next two decades. The resulting consumption boom will drive natural-resource prices higher, opening space for companies that learn to use resources more efficiently." You can find this online at the CNNMoney site. Their angle is, of course, that this will offer opportunities for companies in businesses like "reducing food waste, deploying efficient irrigation systems, and improving the energy efficiency of buildings." And green manufacturing and supply chains? In addition to food and shelter this global middle class is going to be clamouring for all the usual ornaments of that new status; refrigerators, automobiles, televisions, etc.

Do you recall the IPAT equation I have been bandying about in pervious chapter of this book? The basic impact equation (or IPAT, in terms of environmental damage, consumption, etc.) which is simply:

Impact = Population x (GDP/person) x (Impact/GDP)

(And hence the acronym IPAT: I = P x A x T or Impact = Population x Affluence x Technology)

I commented then that population grows with time and most countries strive to improve GDP/capita since that drives living standards, etc. The rate of consumption or environmental impact per unit of GDP is the "rate of damage" done as a result of the technology driving the growth in GDP and is really the only "knob" we can adjust to reduce impact.

I noted that engineers are most effective at changing technology that affects Impact/GDP. To the extent we can reduce that impact we are, effectively, greening the process. And that means we are reducing the impact.

The "business opportunities" in the Fortune article cited in this chapter are addressing this also … but for food production and shelter effectiveness per unit of energy consumed.

I also noted in a later research that not everyone agrees that affluence is a good measure of well-being nor that the GDP/capita is a good measure of either! However, I assume the folks at Fortune would be comfortable with this definition.

Let's look at the concept of Gross National Happiness that comprised a number of logical components as:

1. **Economic Wellness:** economic metrics such as consumer debt, average income to consumer price index ratio and income distribution.
2. **Environmental Wellness:** environmental metrics such as pollution, noise and traffic.
3. **Physical Wellness:** physical health metrics.
4. **Mental Wellness:** mental health metrics such as usage of antidepressants and rise or decline of psychotherapy patients.
5. **Workplace Wellness:** labour metrics such as jobless claims, job change, workplace complaints, etc.
6. **Social Wellness:** discrimination, safety, divorce rates, complaints of domestic conflicts and family lawsuits, public lawsuits, crime rates.
7. **Political Wellness:** political metrics such as the quality of local democracy, individual freedom, and foreign conflicts.

How to characterize these in a practicable way is always the challenge. And, then, how to connect them to some aspect of the design, production, distribution, operation and end of life of our products or systems is even a bit more challenging.

Companies are trying already to become more socially and environmentally responsible organizations. Take Walmart for example. An excellent article on GreenBiz back by Marc Gunther titled "How much of a difference can Walmart really make?" goes into some detail on the activities, and impact of those, on sustainability of one of the world's largest companies (it just got bounced out of the top position, based on sales, by two oil companies!) Based on a careful read and analysis of their recent sustainability report some of Walmart's highlights listed are:

1. Reduced waste by 80 percent.
2. Expanded locally grown produce (up by 97 percent)
3. Pledged to source $20 billion from women-owned businesses in the U.S.
4. Saved customers $1 billion on fresh fruits and vegetables.
5. Announced a "Great for you" icon that will help shoppers identify healthier food items.

The article goes on to say that with respect to waste "Walmart's doing very well, largely because eliminating waste makes business sense. As the new report explains: In 2011, Walmart U.S. prevented 80.9 percent of the waste generated by its stores, clubs and distribution centres nationwide from going to the landfill. This has the potential to prevent more than

11.8 million metric tons of CO2 emissions annually, the equivalent of taking more than 2 million cars off the road. The zero landfill waste program returned more than $231 million to the business in 2011 through a combination of increased recycling revenue and decreased expenses."

Henry Ford would have been pleased. Recall that he said that waste costs you twice; once when you buy the original product or material and the second time when you pay to get rid of the left-overs.

According to the "happiness" list in this chapter some of these clearly have social impacts.

So, the question remains; what are the best (or at least most practicable) social measures and how do we link them to manufacturing (either process improvements for reduction of impact or leveraging for product improvement) and product design?

And, what about trying to influence consumer behaviour? Where does that fit in? It doesn't necessarily mean less profitability!

Chapter 26: Conclusion

Green Manufacturing

The term "green" manufacturing can be looked at in two ways: the manufacturing of "green" products, particularly those used in renewable energy systems and clean technology equipment of all kinds, and the "greening" of manufacturing; reducing pollution and waste by minimizing natural resource use, recycling and reusing what was considered waste, and reducing emissions.

Revitalizing US and UK manufacturing has grown to "rallying cry" levels in recent years, with rapidly growing renewable energy and clean technology investment at the thin end of the wedge. Proponents tout the economic and social benefits of a strong US and UK manufacturing sector while urging government policy makers to enact policies that promote and foster its ongoing development and growth.

At the heart of such calls lay manufacturing's potential to be an engine for long-term job creation and a primary means of assuring US and UK competitiveness across globalized markets in which the US competes with state-managed, "non-market" economies.

US and UK manufacturing has been on the decline as a percentage of GDP for decades. In the 2000s, according to a March 2012 research report from the

Information Technology and Innovation Foundation, "U.S. manufacturing suffered its worst performance in American history in terms of jobs. Not only did America lose 5.7 million manufacturing jobs, but the decline as a share of total manufacturing jobs (33 percent) exceeded the rate of loss in the Great Depression."

Advocates of developing and enacting stronger US government policies and incentives, including the report's authors, lament such statistics and believe it is essential that this trend be reversed. They are coming out publicly, urging leaders to enact policies and take actions to revitalize US and UK manufacturing, firm in the belief that it would be enormously beneficial socially as well as economically. In fact, there's a lot to build on.

The Biggest Manufacturing Country in the World

Despite its decline relative to the services sector, the US manufacturing sector "produces $1.7 trillion of value each year, 11.7% of US GDP," according to the National Association of Manufacturers (NAM). Of late, manufacturing and exports has been a comparative bright spot in a halting, still fragile US economic and jobs recovery.

You might find it surprising, but the US remains the world's largest manufacturing economy, producing 21% of global manufactured products. China is second at 15% and Japan is third at 12%, according to NAM. Pillars for the advent of 21st-century "green" and "zero-carbon" economies, rapidly growing renewable energy and clean tech sectors are considered among the best opportunities to realize this goal.

President Obama and his administration are responding. Spurring a renewal of US manufacturing, and fostering growth in renewable energy and clean technology, are central planks of the President's "Blueprint for an America Built to Last" strategic plan.

Paradigm Shift to Sustainable Capitalism

The challenges facing the planet today are unprecedented and extraordinary; climate change, water scarcity, poverty, disease, growing inequality of income and wealth, demographic shifts, trans-border and internal migration, urbanisation and a global economy in a state of constant dramatic volatility and flux, to name but a few. While governments and civil society will need to be part of the solution to these massive challenges, ultimately it will be companies and investors that will mobilise the capital needed to overcome them.

To address these sustainability challenges, we advocate for a paradigm shift to Sustainable Capitalism; a framework that seeks to maximise long-term economic value creation by reforming markets to address real needs while considering all costs and stakeholders.

One of the objectives of this book is to make the economic case for mainstreaming Sustainable

Capitalism by highlighting the fact that it does not represent a trade-off with profit maximisation but instead actually fosters superior long-term value creation.

We therefore go on to recommend five specific actions that we suggest will accelerate the "mainstreaming of Sustainable Capitalism" by the end of this decade.

1. Identify and Incorporate Risks from Stranded Assets: We define "stranded assets" as "those with a value that would change dramatically, either positively or negatively, under certain scenarios such as a reasonable price on carbon or water, or improved regulation of labour standards in emerging economies.

2. Mandated Integrated Reporting: This is intended to allow more comprehensive insight into companies which is now lacking in spite of increases in the volume of information made available by companies and the frequency with which it is produced.

3. End the Default Practice of Issuing Quarterly Earning Guidance: It has long been argued that relying on quarterly earnings statements creates incentives for short term management at the expense of the longer-term, more meaningful measure of sustainable value creation.

4. Align Compensation Structures with Long-Term Sustainable Performance: Since most current compensation schemes reward short-term actions

disproportionately they fail to hold corporations accountable for the ramifications of their decisions over the long term. Financial rewards should instead be paid out over the period during which these results are realized.

5. Encourage Long-term Investing with Loyalty-Driven Securities: This practice encourage long-term investment horizons among investors and facilitate stability in financial markets, therefore playing an important role in mainstreaming Sustainable Capitalism.

These actions would substantially change the business climate around the world if carried out. What the likelihood of this happening is not known.

The service industry or other non-manufacturing sectors generate less than one dollar of economic activity for every dollar of sector output; unlike manufacturing and agriculture which return more in economic activity than the sector output alone. See the US Government's Bureau of Economic Analysis for more data. Manufacturing and agriculture return $1.35 and $1.20, respectively, in economic activity for every $1 of sector output. Construction, transportation, info tech, finance, etc are less than $1 and as low as $.55 for the retail trade sector.

So, if you want to "leverage" the economy to drive sustainable capitalism; we suggest that you start with manufacturing and agriculture!

Good Luck!